CONTEMPORARY COUNTRY